Feng Shui Made Simple

Feng Shui Made Simple

The Beginner's Guide to Feng Shui for Wealth, Health, and Love

Includes the Five Elements, Finding Your Kua Number, the Lo Pan, Creating a Feng Shui Bedroom, and the Bagua Map

Sabrina Godwin

CAC Publishing

ISBN: 978-1-948489-35-5

Sabrina Godwin

Table of Contents

Introduction to Feng Shui

Feng Shui is an ancient practice that was developed thousands of years ago in China. It is steeped in tradition and based on nature and science. Feng Shui brings a positive balance of energy (also known as having "good chi") to your home, and thus to your life. The words Feng Shui translate to wind and water. In Chinese culture this is associated with good health and good fortune. There are specific Feng shui techniques for bringing good fortune in the form of better health, luck in love, and improving finances. All are based on the belief that the earth is alive with both good and bad energy, or "chi."

It is believed that Feng Shui was first used many thousands of years ago for everything from finding the safest place to build a community to where to plant crops for the most bountiful harvest, and even determining the most appropriate burial site for loved ones who had passed on.

Feng Shui is rooted deeply in Taoism and the belief in positive and negative energy. The philosophy is that if you can optimize the positive energy in your home it will bring good fortune to all who dwell in it and bring harmony to your mind, body and spirit.

Simply stated, in Feng Shui, positive Energy or Chi is created when we are around or creating something esthetically pleasing. Negative Chi or Energy is caused by excessive clutter and things that are ugly.

Just as good Feng Shui can bring good fortune, bad Feng Shui can bring poor health and bad luck.

Yin represents feminine energy and Yang is the masculine energy. The Taoist Yin and Yang symbol represents the fact that one cannot exist without the other. There is no positive without negative and there can be no male without female.

Feng Shui is also associated with nature and the five elements which are also associated with eight directions of the earth. Metal is associated with the East and Northwest, Earth with the Southwest and Northeast, Wood with the East and Southeast, Water with the North, and last, Fire with the South. It is believed that when we are born, our time and place of birth creates a specific energy and that this energy can shape our lives.

2

Yin and Yang

The symbol of Yin and Yang shows the perfect balance between two opposite energies that cannot exist without the other. They are shown as two parts of the same circle. The feminine energy is represented by black. It has a white (masculine,) circle in it to represent its connection. The Yang color is white but has a little black circle in it. Both Yin and Yang are shown in one larger circle representing the universe.

The female Yin energy is considered a quiet and passive energy. The deep black color represents night time, relaxation and slow movement.

Yang is active, masculine energy. It is the energy that we use as we go about our day.

The color white in Feng Shui represents the element Metal and is a representation of purity.

White should be used in your home in areas where the dominant element is metal. This is the West and Northwest facing sides of your residence. Using all white in West and Northwest facing sides can bring peace and tranquility. Do not use white as the main color in the East or South East facing sides of your home as this would cause negative energy. It is fine to use white as an accent to other colors on these sides but never as your main color.

Black should be used in the North, East and Southeast facing side of your home, although it should only be used sparingly inside. North symbolizes water and East and Southeast represent woods. If used in large amounts it can cause an oppressive feeling. Black is a color of power, protection and the element of water. It encourages stability in your life. If used in North facing sides, it can attract new job opportunities. Use it sparingly indoors and have it at or below eye level. Black-trimmed pillows or accent rugs would be a good example, or a mirror set into a black frame. Black should not be used in South facing areas. Avoid it's use in dining areas, kitchens and especially keep it out of children's bedrooms.

The Five Elements

There are five basic elements that effect energy in positive and negative ways. They are Wood, Fire, Metal, Earth and Water. Each element also has assigned colors and directions to be used with Feng Shui. Each element has cycles which are positive or negative. The elements can support each other or obstruct each other, which, in turn, can have a constructive or destructive outcome. When used in a harmonious way, positive energy can flow freely. When the elements are used in a way that causes their energy to clash, it will cause a destructive cycle which can cause conflict.

The productive cycle is as follows:

Fire Fosters Earth
Earth Fosters Metal
Metal Fosters Water
Water Fosters Wood
Wood Fosters Fire

The destructive cycle would be:
Fire Destroys Metal

Earth Destroys Water

Metal Destroys Wood

Water Destroys Fire

Wood Destroys Earth

The way the elements react to each other depends on its harmonic interactive factor with that element. Their rapport produces positive or negative energy.

By utilizing this rapport between the elements, you can bring positive energy into your home. You can also remove any destructive energy that may already be present. Every element has specific colors and directions.

Element	**Energy Type**	**Color**	**Direction**
Fire	Yang Active	Red, Orange	South
Earth	Neutral Energy	Yellow, Beige, Brown	Center Dominant, Southwest, Northwest
Water	Yin Energy	Dark Blue, Black	North
Metal	Yin and Yang	White or Gold	West
Wood	Yin and Yang	Green	East

The following are the Elements that have a natural connection and are compatible with each other. They work together to create positive energy.

Water helps Wood (water helps plants and trees to grow)

Wood helps Fire (Wood helps fire to Burn)

Fire produces Dust (Earth)

Earth helps Mineral (Metal) to form

Metal can hold Water.

Water is Wood's supportive element;

Wood releases the influence of Water.

Wood is the supportive component of Fire.

Fire releases the influence of Wood.

Fire is the supportive element for Earth.

Earth releases the influence of Fire.

Earth is the supportive element of Metal.

Metal releases the influence of Earth.

Metal is the supportive element of Water.

Water releases the influence of Metal.

Elements that oppose each other are destructive and create negative energy. Because they are in conflict, it negates the positive energy they would both otherwise create. The elements that are destructive to each other are as follows:

Water smothers Fire,

Fire dissolves Water

Wood breakdowns the ground (Earth),

Earth entombs Wood

Fire liquifies Metal but

Metal is not liquified until Fire is smothered.

Earth absorbs Water but

Water can overflow the Earth.

Metal cuts Wood but

becomes dull before the Wood is cut.

Water and Fire are adversaries.

Water breaks the liveliness of Fire.

Wood and Earth are adversaries.

Wood blocks the dynamism of Earth.

Fire and Metal are adversaries.

Fire overpowers the movement of Metal.

Earth and Water are adversaries.

Earth overpowers the movement of Water.

Metal and Wood are adversaries.

Metal overpowers the movement of Wood.

These elements do not work in sync with each other. They block each other's positive energy. When incorporating Feng Shui never put two elements that are inharmonious together. If you do, it will encourage negative energy instead of positive energy.

The Characteristics of the Elements

Fire - is a lively, aggressive energy. Colors which symbolize fire are bright and brilliant. Oranges, reds, purples and pinks all represent fire. These colors promote growth and change. The shapes associated with the element of fire are diamonds, pyramids, sunbursts and triangles. These shapes send high speed energy in all directions, which encourages movement and transformation. In Feng Shui, Fire energy is for hard work, expanding job opportunities, increased prosperity, and love. The direction of fire is South.

Earth - is a supportive and quiet energy. The colors that represent Earth are more subdued; Yellow, Beige, Brown - muted earth tones. These are colors of slow and relaxing quiet energy. The shapes associated with the earth element are rectangles and squares. These are considered grounding shapes. Choosing artwork for your home that is in landscape shape rather than portrait can increase earth energy. The earth element brings a feeling of stability and security to the family. The direction of Earth is center dominant, Southwest or Northwest.

Wood - is associated with the energy of personal growth. The colors for wood are green, sometimes with small amounts of purple. Wood represents upward moving energy. The shapes associated with wood are cylinders and columns. Wood infuses the home with oxygen and is related to good health and prosperity. Its direction is East.

Water- is the element of new beginnings. A kind of out with the old and in with the new. Its colors are dark blue to black. Water energy brings wisdom. The shape for this energy is symbolized by any shape that is flowing or that can hold water. When water flows it is a symbol of being bountiful. Using the energy of the water element in your home will purify it. The direction for Water is North.

Metal – is the element for energy of the mind. The colors for metal are white, silver, gray and gold. This energy is associated with intelligence and creativity. Its shape symbol is the circle. The energy of metal can bring efficiency to the home and clarity to the mind. Its direction is West.

All of the elements have a Yin or Yang energy. There are even times that it can possess both. Yin Metal would be pliant silver that bends while Yang metal is unbending steel. Plants that are green and robust are considered Yang, while dried or woody plants are Yin. Paintings of water and wavy curtains are Yin energy, but fountains and streams are Yang. Fire is Yang, but soft shimmery candles are Yin.

In terms of Feng Shui, when you learn the concept of harmonious and inharmonious elements you can use them in your home. If you were born under a fire element year you should not use many water energy objects or colors in your home because Water destroys Fire. So, for this example, you would not use black or dark blue. You would not want a water fountain in your home. What would be good for someone born under Fire energy would be to use a lot of wood elements in your home, because wood feeds fire. Since Fires direction is south, you would want to choose a south facing bedroom, if possible.

Your Element and Direction based on the hour of your birth.

Time	Element	Direction
11pm to 1am	Wood	North
1am to 3am	Wood	North and Northeast
3am to 5am	Fire	East to Northeast
5am to 7am	Fire	East
7am to 9am	Earth	East to Southeast
9am to 11am	Earth	South to Southeast
11am to 1pm	Metal	South
1pm to 3pm	Metal	South to Southeast
3pm to 5pm	Water	West to Southwest
5pm to 7pm	Water	West to Southwest
7pm to 9pm	Water	West to Northwest
9pm to 11pm	Water	North to Northwest

Check your Element against the Year of Your Birth

Rat

- 1972 Water
- 1984 Wood
- 1996 Fire
- 1960 Metal
- 1948 Earth
- 1936 Fire
- 1924 Wood
- 1900 Metal

Ox

- 1997 Fire
- 1985 Wood
- 1973 Water
- 1961 Metal
- 1949 Earth
- 1937 Fire
- 1925 Wood
- 1913 Water
- 1901 Metal

Tiger

- 1998 Earth
- 1986 Fire
- 1974 Wood
- 1962 Water
- 1950 Metal
- 1938 Earth,
- 1926 Fire
- 1914 Wood
- 1902 Water

Rabbit

- 1999 Earth
- 1987 Fire
- 1975 Wood
- 1963 Water
- 1951 Metal
- 1939 Earth
- 1927 Fire
- 1915 Wood
- 1903 Water

Dragon

- 2000 Metal
- 1988 Earth
- 1976 Fire
- 1964 Wood
- 1952 Water
- 1940 Metal
- 1928 Earth
- 1916 Fire
- 1904 Wood

Snake

- 2001 Metal
- 1989 Earth
- 1977 Fire
- 1965 Wood
- 1953 Water
- 1941 Metal
- 1929 Earth
- 1917 Fire
- 1905 Wood

Horse

- 2002 Water
- 1990 Metal
- 1978 Earth
- 1966 Fire
- 1954 Wood
- 1942 Water
- 1930 Metal
- 1918 Earth
- 1906 Fire

Monkey

- 2003 Water
- 1991 Metal
- 1979 Earth
- 1967 Fire
- 1955 Wood
- 1943 Water
- 1931 Metal
- 1919 Earth
- 1907 Fire

Rooster

- 2005 Wood
- 1993 Water
- 1981 Metal
- 1969 Earth
- 1957 Fire
- 1945 Wood
- 1933 Water
- 1921 Metal
- 1908 Earth

Dog

- 2006 Fire
- 1994 Wood
- 1982 Water
- 1970 Metal
- 1958 Earth
- 1946 Fire
- 1934 Wood
- 1922 Water
- 1909 Metal

Boar

- 2007 Fire
- 1995 Wood
- 1983 Water
- 1971 Metal
- 1959 Earth
- 1947 Fire
- 1935 Wood
- 1923 Water
- 1910 Metal

In Feng Shui, the elements are used to create a positive flow of Qi (energy) in our home which, in turn, enhances our internal energy. A Fire element person could, for example, put red objects in the direction that will bring Yang energy to that area. If space is limited, even a red or orange candle will suffice.

Earth energy is soothing and nourishing. It can improve marriage and relationships. Objects and colors representing earth should be placed in the southwest direction to bring closeness and intimacy.

Metal is a Yang element. An easy way to remember Yin and Yang is that hard things are considered Yang and soft are considered Yin. If you have too much Yin energy in one area you can balance it with Yang by adding a metal object. Using chimes in water areas can help to blend the Yin and Yang energies.

Water is the element of prosperity. If water objects are added to Northern areas, which are the direction for job opportunities, it can cause a positive outcome in career goals.

Placing a water element in a wealth direction is beneficial. Do not use water elements in bedrooms or bathrooms. Because water represents wealth, you would not want to use this where water is running down a drain or being flushed away. If you have a large yard with room to place a fountain in a direction of wealth it will stimulate positive energy flow.

Wood represents both Yin and Yang energy. The comingling of the two energies is what creates trees. Wood is associated with prosperity and health.

As we discussed earlier, every element has colors and direction. The element of Fire and the direction of South can produce positive energy towards bringing you recognition for your work. Using the fire colors of red, orange, pink, and purple in the south direction of your office or home can increase the energy of fame and recognition, which can be positive for your career.

Using green in the direction of east can bring energy that improves health and family life. Blue can be used in a North direction to compliment your career plans or in the East for health and family. If you use blue in a South-East direction it helps to nourish the Wood element which can bring an increase in prosperity.

Using Yellow in a South direction can bring increased happiness. White in a Western direction can increase your imagination and mental clarity.

The following is a summary of the elements.

Fire: Red: South =

Fame and Reputation

Lights, candles, artwork, throw pillows, accent rugs using red. Fire and Red are Yang energy. Yang is energizing.

Earth: Earth Yellow: Ochre: Beige to Brown: Earth Tone Colors and Materials: Southwest/Northeast/Center =

Schooling and Knowledge

Terra-cotta, ceramics, porcelain, plants placed in terra-cotta or ceramic containers.

Metal: Pewter, Silver & Gold: West & Northwest =

Nurtures Imagination and Children

Metal candle holders, picture frames, decorations, ceremonial dinner dishes with silver or gold trim. Metal kitchen appliances, watering cans and/or decorations in the West bend of your garden.

Water: North =

Career

Aquariums, fountains, ponds.

When we begin to use the ideas behind Feng Shui we start to see positive changes. Even the littlest things like replacing a vase with a different color creates a difference in the energy you are circulating in your home.

Finding Your Kua Number

To utilize Feng Shui accurately you need to know your Kua Number. Your Kua number will determine the appropriate compass directions for your home called "Auspicious Directions". It also tells you the directions that are negative to you called the "Inauspicious Directions." It is by using the appropriate directions determined by your Kua number that nurtures the flow of Qi (positive energy) in your space. The Kua number. which is also called Gua, allows you to locate the 4 directions of a room or area.

To figure out your Kua number, you will use your gender and birth year.

1. Take the year of your birth and add the last two digits.

    For instance: If you were born in 1957 add 5+7=12

2. Next take the number and reduce it to one number. Example: 12 is broken into two separate digits that are added together. 12 = 1+2=3

The next calculation will depend on your gender. If you are female add 5 to your number. For the example we were using it would be 3, so 3+5=8.

If your birth number was a 5 and you add 5, getting 10, you reduce the number to a single digit as in step 1. So in this case 5+5 =10 = 1+0 =1 and the Kua female number would be 1. So, to get the female Kua number you add 5 to the birth year after reducing it to a single digit.

For a Male Kua Number

1. Step one is the same; so, if the birth year is 1957, for a male you also add the last two digits together and then reduce to a single digit. ex. 5+7 =12, 1+2=3

2. For a male, you subtract the single birth year from the number 10. So, in this case 10-3=7. The male Kua number in this example is 7.

Now that you have your Kua number you will use it to determine if your direction is East or West.

EAST Group Kua Numbers are:

Kua Number 9

Kua Number 4

Kua Number 3

Kua Number 1

WEST Group Kua Numbers are:

Kua Number 8

Kua Number 7

Kua Number 6

Kua Number 5

Kua Number 2

*There are Feng Shui schools that don't use the number 5. That being the case, females would replace the number 5 with Kua 8 and males replace 5 with Kua

Kua 1:

Favorable Southeast Unfavorable West

Kua 2:

Favorable Northeast Unfavorable East

Kua 3:

Favorable South Unfavorable Southeast

Kua 4:

Favorable North Unfavorable Northwest

Kua 5:

Favorable Northeast Unfavorable East

Kua 5:

Female Favorable Northeast Unfavorable East

Kua 6:

Favorable West Unfavorable Southeast

Kua 7:

Favorable Northwest Unfavorable North

Kua 8:

Favorable Southwest Unfavorable South

Kua 9:

Favorable East Unfavorable Northeast

BaGua

Another tool in Feng Shui is Ba Gua or BaGua. The Ba Gua is an octagonal grid which holds the symbols of the I Ching. The sections of the octagon have an I Ching symbol which pertains to a direction on a compass. Ba Gua shows you how to use the spaces in and around your home and the ways they relate to everyday life. It is used to analyze the Qi of certain spaces in your home. Ba translates to 8 and Gua translates to trigram. Together they make 8 areas. So, the BaGua is a chart of the 8 directions and what they symbolize.

First, you will require a compass. You can use a western compass or the traditional Feng Shui compass known as lo pan. The main difference between them being that Lo Pan uses South while a Western compass points North. Each of the 8 areas on the Ba Gua Grid has its own direction, element, color and area of life associated with it.

Here are some examples of Ba Gua Grids.

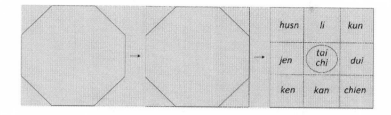

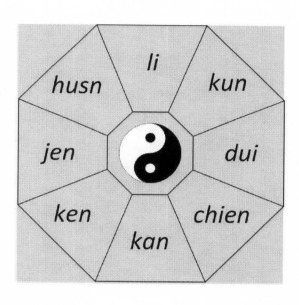

The 8 areas have I Ching names and meanings. Each area is called Gua. Each Gua has a certain I Ching Symbol called Yao. Each Yao is a diagram of Yin and Yang energy and the ways in which they interact. The two short lines are feminine or Yin. The solid line is Yang or male. The Yin lines correspond to the number Zero 0 and the Yang line to the number one 1.

Here is a description of each of the BaGua areas in terms of the I Ching Symbols or Yao.

KUN

The area farthest in the upper right corner symbolizes the Earth. It represents the female, mother. Mother symbolizes the origin of life. The direction is southwest and element is earth.

Zhen/Jen

The area left in the middle of the Yao Hsun and Ken. Zhen means thunder. Its direction is East and symbolizes Health and Family. Its element is Wood

Li

Li is the top Yao. It means Fire. Li is the South Direction. It represents Fame and Reputation. It is also called the illumination area because fame and reputations can illuminate us. The element for this area is Fire.

Dui

The middle right area between Yao Kun and Chien is Dui. It symbolizes Children and Creativity and its direction is West. This area brings joy, imagination and romance. The element for this area is Metal.

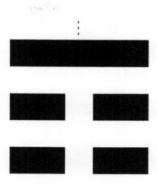

Ken/Gen

This is the farthest lower left corner. Gen means mountain and represents Knowledge, Cultivation, and Spirituality. Its direction is Northeast and element is earth.

Kan

This is Kan which means Water. Its direction is the opposite of Li which is North. This area symbolizes Career or job opportunities and its element is Water.

Xun

The word Xun means the wind. This area corresponds to Wealth and Prosperity. The direction is Southeast and element is Wood.

Qian/Chien

This is the Gua where the transformation of Yin to Yang is complete. It is the most powerful of the Yang and opposite of Kun. It is the farthest lower right corner of the chart. It symbolizes the king, the father, the emperor, the boss and the Alpha male. This direction is Northwest and represents helpful people and travel. The element is Metal.

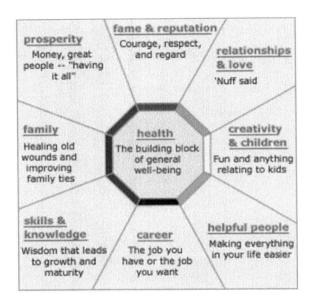

prosperity	fame & reputation	relationships
Money, great people -- "having it all"	Courage, respect, and regard	& love 'Nuff said

family	health	creativity
Healing old wounds and improving family ties	The building block of general well-being	& children Fun and anything relating to kids

skills & knowledge	career	helpful people
Wisdom that leads to growth and maturity	The job you have or the job you want	Making everything in your life easier

The Lo Pan or Chinese Compass

The LoPan, or Compass, that is used in Feng Shui. Lo means "Everything". Pan Means "Bowl", and together they are interpreted to mean a tool that can receive access to the mysteries of the universe. The Lo Pan or the Feng Shui compass is a metal compass that has concentric directional rings around a magnetic needle. In most compasses the metal part is set on a wooden base which symbolizes earth. The base is usually red. In Chinese culture red is considered favorable as well as protective.

The Feng Shui Lo Pan doesn't point North like a Western Compass. The Chinese Compass points South with its starting point 0. The literal translation for the word of the needle that does the pointing in the Lo Pan is "Needle that points South".

There are three types of Feng Shui compasses They are the San He, the San Yuan and the Flying Star. All three compasses have some formula rings in common. They include the 24 mountains and the heavens. Some Feng Shui masters make their own compasses. A professional Feng Shui compass can have more than 40 rings of information on it.

Originally, a Lo Pan was made from tiger bone and painted by hand. These days you can purchase a Lo Pan in Feng Shui Markets or over the internet. Not every Feng Shui compass is accurate, so you must know which one to buy. You need not be a Feng Shui Master to use a Feng Shui compass, but you do need an accurate compass to do Feng Shui. This is a diagram of a typical Feng Shui Compass:

To practice Feng Shui, you should become familiar with the 24 mountains. The 24 mountains are the 24 sub directions in nearly every Feng Shui compass. These formulas are condensed on the Lo Pan into one ring around the whole compass. Each of the 24 mountains are divided into 15-degree segments. If you were to multiply the 15 X 24 you get 360 degrees which is the circumference of the compass circle.

The sub directions are based on the Eight Mansions and Flying Star. The Eight Mansions are 8 Gua numbers which are calculated to find your Kua number. The system is commonly referred to as Ba Zhai or Eight Mansions. With Eight Mansions, Qi flow is analyzed through cycles. Flying Star is a term used for the flow of lucky Qi. The Eight Mansions and Flying Star are the foundation of the Water Dragon formulas and other sub formulas created from the main Flying Star formula. The reason the compass is useful is because Feng Shui characterizes buildings according to the direction they face when being built. You can use a western compass to get the directions also. The western compass always finds North as a starting point while the Lo Pan starts with South.

Here are the Specific Directions, Elements, Colors and Areas Associated with each of the Feng Shui Ba Gua locations according to compass directions.

*In Feng Shui, remember that the 0 degree is the South Direction.

North

Compass Reading 337.5 to 22.5

Water Element

Colors are Blue & Black

Life Area: Career

Life Path: Fame

Northeast

Compass Reading - 22.5 to 67.5

Earth Element

Colors are Light Yellow, Beige & Sandy

Life Area: Spiritual Development & Self- Cultivation

East

Compass Reading - 67.5 to 112.5

Wood Element

Colors are Brown & Green

Life Area: Well-Being & Family

Southeast

Compass Reading - 112.5 to 157.5

Wood Element

Colors are Brown & Green

Life Area: Cash & Wealth

South

Compass Reading - 157.5 to 202.5

Fire Element

Colors are Red, Orange, Purple, Pink & Bright Yellow

Life Area: Celebrity & Character

Southwest

Compass Reading - 202.5 to 247.5

Earth Element

Colors are Beige, Light Yellow, & Sandy/Earthy

Life Area: Love and Marital

West

Compass Reading - 247.5 to 292.5

Metal Element

Colors are White and Grey

Life Area: Imagination and Children

The Bagua

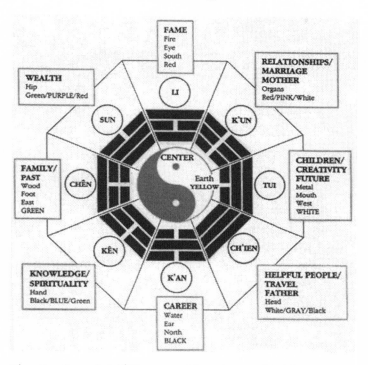

The Ba Gua Grid/Chart or Map is used with your Kua number to determine your favorable directions on the compass. The Ba Gua determines the spaces in your area. It has 8 spaces and the Ba Gua is either in squares or an octagonal shape. Each of the spaces corresponds to an area of your life. Using the grid as a guide, you assess each living space in corresponding aspects to the grid.

Bagua Map for Eastern Feng Shui

This is used for your home or business as a whole.

	Wealth and Prosperity	Fame and Reputation	Love and Marriage
Location	SE corner	S corner	SW Corner
Colors	Purples, Reds, Greens	Reds and Oranges	Reds, Pinks, Whites

	Health and Family	Earth YOU	Creativity and Children
Location	E Corner	Center	W Corner
Colors	Blues and Greens	Yellows and Earth tones	Metals, White and pastels

	Knowledge and Self Cultivation	Career	Helpful People and Travel
Location	NE Corner	N Corner	NW Corner
Colors	Black, Blues, Greens	Black and Dark Blues	White, Gray, Black

The Elements

    South-Fire

    East-Wood

    North-Water

    West-Metal

    Center-Earth

Bagua Map for Western Feng Shui

This map is based on individual rooms of your home or business.

	Wealth and Prosperity	Fame and Reputation	Love and Marriage
Location	Rear Left	Rear Middle	Rear Right
Colors	Purples, Reds, Greens	Reds, Oranges	Reds, Pinks, White

	Health and Family	Earth YOU	Creativity and Children
Location	Middle Left	Center	Middle Right
Colors	Blues, Greens	Yellows and Earth tones	Pastels and White

	Knowledge and Self Cultivation	Career	Helpful People and Travel
Location	Front Left	Front Middle	Front Right
Colors	Black, Blues	Black and Dark Blues	White, Gray, Black

Entrance

Entrance to your rooms or offices will be in one of the three front areas of Knowledge and Cultivation, Career or Helpful People and Travel

Elements

    Family and Reputation: Fire

    Health and Family: Wood

    Career: Water

    Creativity and Children: Metal

    Center (YOU): Earth

For Missing Bagua Areas

Obviously not all of us have houses or apartments that match all the parts of the Bagua Map. When this occurs, we say that the Bagua is incomplete and the energy is weak. In many cases it's not that the areas are missing, but that they are smaller in comparison to others. When areas are small or missing it is considered, in Feng Shui, to be out of balance or negative. This is said to create an energy void or weak spot in the Bagua of a home. These areas are called Bagua void areas, Bagua negative areas or Bagua weak areas. An example of a missing Bagua area would be not having a "Career Area" Bagua in your home according to the Bagua Map. In this case, you would need to compensate for those weak areas to correct the negative energy.

When weak or negative energy is corrected in Feng Shui it is called cures. Cures strengthen the positive energy flow and balance the area that is lacking. The center of the BaGua, which is the heart, cannot be missing. When you understand the five elements and directions you can use simple cures like mirrors, colors, or fountains to increase the Qi in the weak area.

Tips for the Missing Bagua Locations

North - The Bagua area associated with the north is Career. The element for the north is water. Remedies or cures for this missing Direction would either be water or nurturing elements like metal.

Things that help for a weak North location are large round or oval mirrors, artwork in black and white, or bringing in water, like a flowing fountain. Wall murals with deep blues of the sky and sea can bring positive energy in this direction, or even just painting the wall blue.

The animal that represents the North is the Black Turtle. The turtle is a symbol of long life, endurance and strength. In Feng Shui, the black turtle symbolizes hills behind a dwelling. The hills represent support and protection. In most houses, the front door faces south and the back faces North. (Remember, in Feng Shui Our

51

North is their South). In this case the black turtle represents the back of the building.

Missing Northeast Bagua

Earth (or Fire since fire nourishes the earth) is the element to cure missing Northeastern Bagua.

This direction is associated with spirituality and personal growth. It is also the location of the divine presence your life. If you have weak Northeast Bagua you should use artwork that has pictures of mountains or other earth elements, and items that reflect your own spirituality. Candles and all fire colors are also helpful in this area. Water and Metal elements are both to be avoided in this direction.

Missing East Bagua

Wood is the element of the east and water can strengthen wood. Your cures for this direction should utilize these elements. This Bagua direction is associated with Life and Family. It is important to maximize Qi flow in this area to optimize health on all levels. Health is defined as physical, mental, emotional and spiritual. Included in health are aspects of harmonious energy to maintain peace in the family.

Wooden furniture, plants and artwork should be used in this direction. Pictures showing happy and healthy families can be good here. Water element objects will also strengthen the energy of wood. Square or rectangular mirrors in wooden frames can bring positive energy here, as will using colors of wood and water. Fire and Metal elements should not be used in this area.

The animal that represents the East is the green dragon. The green dragon signifies protection for all who reside there. Hills that represent the green dragon are higher than those of the white tiger behind the home. The green dragon is Yang energy. It represents strength, goodness, courage and endurance. He is anything symbolizing vigilance and security. The white tiger of the west is inseparable from the green dragon.

Missing South East Bagua

This area is related to Prosperity and Abundance. The element related to this Bagua is Wood. This area needs

Wood elements and Water reinforcements when it is missing or weak. It is recommended to express prosperity and all its forms in this directional area. This means both the material wealth and the blessings of life. Use this direction to show abundance. Pictures showing what wealth means to you, both emotionally and materially, can be used here. Shapes should be square for wood or wavy to symbolize flowing water that nurtures the wood.

Fire or Metal should not be used here. Walls can be painted in greens, browns, blues and black. Mirrors in wooden frames will cure this area as well.

Missing South Bagua

The elements of the south are Fire and the Wood which nourishes the Fire. To strengthen the weak and missing area of Fame and Reputation use Fire and Wood elements. The translation for this Bagua area is "the light within". In this area you want to use elements that show what light you bring to the world, what is the essence of your reputation. Use artwork and other objects that speak to your heart about what you want to be known for.

Candles in fire colors and wooden furniture are appropriate for this area. The colors you should use are reds, pinks, purples, oranges and strong yellows for the Fire, and greens and browns for the wood. Use triangular shapes for the fire element and squares and rectangles for the wood. Tall lights are also good to strengthen this area. Lights are a form of fire. Do not use Water elements in a Southern area. A fireplace is a favorable cure for a Southern Bagua. You can also paint the walls in any of the fire or wood colors.

The Red Phoenix is the animal of this direction. It protects the front of the home and is a sign of luxury. In Chinese mythology the frame of the Phoenix signifies the 5 human qualities. The head signifies virtue, the wings signifies duty, the back means correct behavior, the breast means mortality and the stomach means dependability.

Missing West Bagua

This is the direction of Children and Creativity. The elements of this direction are Metal and its nurturing element, Earth. In this direction it's important to have objects reflecting your creative endeavors as well as support for the energy of your children. Use artwork and objects made from the metal element as well as the earth element here.

Place pictures of your children here, or artwork and items that your children have made. Do not use Fire or water elements here. Tall lighting is a plus in this area. The colors are shades of gray or white and earth colors which are yellows, beige and earth tones. The shapes that strengthen this area are Round and Oval, for metal and square, and rectangular for earth. Paint the walls in Metal and Earth colors in this area.

The white tiger is the animal that represents this direction. White tiger is Yin, passive and feminine but provides protection from the evil intent of strangers. It is inseparable from the dragon.

Missing Northwest Bagua

This is the Bagua of Helpful People/Blessings and Travel. The elements for this direction are Metal and Earth. Use objects in this direction that reflect things to attract helpful people in your life. You should also use items that express your gratitude for the helpful energy you already receive in your life. Do not use Fire or Water objects in this direction. This is a good area to place pictures of destinations you have traveled to, or that you hope to travel to, and photos of positive people in your life.

Tall lights and sculptures are helpful in this direction. Round objects for Metal and Square for earth should be used here. White, gray earth tones, yellows and beiges are the best color choices in this area.

There are tips to make each area of the Bagua map favorable for you. Since clutter blocks the flow of positive energy keep all spaces neat and free of clutter.

Bagua for Wealth and Prosperity

This is the Southeast corner of your home or business. In an individual room, it is the rear left section of the Bagua. Use this area to increase your finances, or to bring abundance to your life. Abundance means more than material things. It can be an abundance of love, friends or whatever it is you need more of in your life. Think of what you want and use this area to bring those desires to fruition.

Favorable tips for this area

1. Favorable colors for this area are red, purple and green.

2. Tying three Chinese coins with a red ribbon and placing them in this corner is favorable. If you do so, make sure the coins are in increments of 3, 6 or 8. 8 is the most powerful money manifestation.

3. Hang a chime from the ceiling to promote wisdom and good Qi.

4. Water objects keep money flowing. Use a picture of flowing water.

5. A fish tank or bowl in the wealth corner promotes financial growth. As your fish grow so does your money from that corner.

6. If you have a backyard and it slopes downward in the south-eastern corner away from the house, then put a light fixture there. Shine it towards the house and you symbolically guide money towards your home.

7. Place a windmill, weather vane, a pin wheel, or any spinning thing in the far-left corner of your

back yard. This stimulates the movement of air and Qi and attracts wealth.

8. Plants which grow slow represent slow growing wealth.

9. The wealth area is in the far-left corner of a room. Put 3 plants together with round leaves in those areas. Round leaves signify coins. If they bare red or purple flowers, even better.

10. Plug all drains in the home when not using them. This symbolizes the idea of preventing money from going down the drain.

11. Keep the toilet seat down when not in use. This reinforces the idea of not letting money go down the toilet.

12. Use earth tones in rooms that have an abundance of water, like bathrooms and kitchens. The color is like a damn to keep your money in.

13. Keep the stove clean. Food is connected to wealth.

14. Hang or place a mirror above or behind the stove so it reflects twice as many burners as before.

Make sure your doors open all the way in your home so as not to limit your possibilities of wealth and living in comfort and ease.

1. Place 3 similar objects in either the wealth area of your living room or bedroom. Try to use gold, purple, red and green.

2. Keep valuables, coin collections, piggy banks, safes, jewelry and things you value in the far-left corner in your bedroom. This amplifies the wealth you collect.

Bagua for Fame and Reputation

This is the Southern corner of your home or business. In individual rooms, it is the rear middle BaGua area. Fame isn't limited to career. A job that we work to pay the rent is not necessarily what we want to do with our lives. A person can work as a driver but have aspirations of being an actor. So, in this area you would place objects that symbolize what you want to become, not necessarily the job you already have. Use this location to express who you want to be and not what others expect you to be.

Here are some tips for the Fame and Reputation Area:

1. Use red for objects in a room in this area as well as in the Southern corner or rear middle area of your home. Red activates the fame and reputation energy. Red area rugs, pillows, vases, etc. should be used here.

2. Fire element objects work well in this area, too. Candles, fireplace incense, paintings.

3. Wood element nourishes fire, so wood can be used here.

4. Display things of merit that you have earned like diplomas, awards, trophies.

5. This area should have bright lights.

6. Keep something in this area that you would like to be known for. It is fine to use a photograph or painting,

7. Use physical reminders of your goals, like charts, to keep you focused. It will direct positive energy towards your goal.

Display something that shows unselfishness or charity here. When you help others, it promotes good Chi

Bagua for Love and Marriage

The Love and Relationships/Marriage area is the South-Western corner of your home or business. In an individual room, it is the right rear section of the Bagua. You can attract new love or enhance your current love in this area.

Tips to Enhance this Bagua area:

1. Hang pictures of you and your spouse/partner.

2. Place a pair of objects in this corner, one representing you and one representing your spouse/partner, like a pair of animals who mate for life. This represents successful partnering. Place them in the rear far right corner or the southwest corner of the bedroom.

3. Mandarin Ducks are a symbol of lovers and marital bliss. Using a pair of ducks in the South-Western corner of your home or in the far-right corner of your living room or bedroom promotes love energy.

4. Cover mirrors in your bedroom. A mirror facing the bed may cause failure in the relationship.

5. TVs should not be in the bedroom.

6. Place the bed where it is not in direct line with the door. Do not have your feet facing the door. This is considered bad Qi. They take the dead from the bedroom feet first.

7. Do not place the bed under a window.

8. Your bed should be accessible from three sides, this creates positive love and energy to attract, or keep, a spouse or partner.

9. Bedrooms should be peaceful, they are meant for sleeping and making love. Do not keep items of violence here such as guns or dark artwork. Also remove exercise equipment. The bedroom should not be a place of hard work.

10. Hang a picture of Peonies in the living room on the south wall to symbolize love.

11. Remove any objects that remind you of work from the bedroom.

12. Do not keep anything under the bed as it can cause arguing between you and your spouse/partner.

13. Burn two red candles in the southwest corner for a few minutes every night to invoke love.

14. Use beads and fabrics.

15. Pink crystals or wind chimes in a sunny window produce positive energy to being love.

16. Plant two fruit bearing trees in the right corner of your back yard. It symbolizes a fruitful relationship.

17. If you are not able to plant fruit bearing trees in this area place a table and 2 chairs in this location. Put fresh flowers on the table often.

18. Use the colors of love and romance here. Pink, red, and white.

19. Make a wish list of all the things you want to attract in a mate. Spend several minutes a day reading your list. Picture yourself meeting your ideal spouse.

Bagua for Health and Family

This is the East corner of your home or Business. In individual rooms, this is the middle-left section of the Bagua. This is the Bagua of New beginnings, health issues, family and friends who are like family.

Blues and Greens should be used here. Here are some tips:

1. Hang pictures of family and friends in this area. If there are three people in a photo, make sure they are staggered. Three people in a line side by side is bad Feng Shui.
2. Keep books on herbs and healing.
3. Clear crystals give the room a rainbow, which is good Qi health energy. Rose crystals are good for emotional Qi. Green Crystals are good for physical health Qi. Blue crystals promote mental clarity.
4. Wood nurtures this area. Wooden furniture and mirrors, or photos in wood frames, should be used here.

5. Objects that make you think of family and close friends are good in this area. Anything you have inherited from loved ones should go here.

6. This is where to place your exercise equipment.

7. Consider getting a pet. Pets stimulate life force energy and symbolize unconditional love.

8. Souvenirs, or anything that reminds you of good times you have had, should go here.

9. Burn incense, oils, or scented candles.

10. Wear green to symbolize health.

11. Wear pink to remove anger.

12. Use items that represent longevity like tortoises, or any plant or animal that lives a long life.

Bagua for You/The Earth

The center of the Bagua is called the You, or Earth Area. In your home or business, it is the center; in individual room,s it's the center of the Bagua. This area is a representation of you in relation to the world.

Tips for this Bagua

1. Ask yourself what you want. Listen to your inner voice and what it is telling you. Write it down.

2. Try to see changes in your life as adventures, not annoyances.

3. Meditate or practice yoga. Listen to music and dance. Feel the joy of just being alive.

Bagua for Creativity and Children

This is the West corner of your Business or Home. In individual rooms, it is the middle right area of the Bagua. This location is about creativity and coming up with ideas. It is also for improving relationships with your children.

Tips for Enhancing this BaGua Area

1. This is the best location for arts and crafts and all creative projects.

2. TV's, stereos and computers can be placed here.

3. Photos of family and friends should go here, along with items of sentimental value.

4. Keep fresh flowers here; especially in pink or white, which are the favorable colors here.

5. Keep things to remind you of your goals and dreams here.

6. This is a good place to keep your pet items.

Bagua for Knowledge and Self-Cultivation

This Bagua area is the northeastern corner of your business or home. In an individual room, this would be the left front of the Bagua map. This area characterizes our longing to know and to learn more. This BaGua is about growing our minds.

Tips for This Bagua Area:

The Enhancing Colors for this Area: Blues, Greens and Black

1. This is a good location for a book case reflecting your interests and a globe for increased interest in the world as a whole.

2. Keep anything related to writing here. Desk, pens, paper etc. This area should also have bright lighting and a comfortable chair.

3. Red activates educational success. Use red in the Southeastern section of this area.

4. This area can benefit from items made of clay. A vase, pot, ashtray or anything clay related is good here.

5. Windchimes can be used here, but they must not be metal.

6. Any object that represents knowledge or growth; like plants and educational books.

Bagua for Career

The Bagua area that encourages career aspirations is the North corner of your home or business. In an individual room, this area is the front middle section of the Bagua.

Tips for Enhancing this Bagua Area

Enhancing Colors for this Bagua Area: Blues and Black

1. Chimes outside the front door is good Qi for a promotion or job opportunities.

2. Brightly colored flags, windsocks or banners can be placed here.

3. A bird bath or bird feeder attracts positive energy.

4. Make a list of things you would like to do if money was not a factor.

5. Keep a colorful welcome mat at your front door.

6. If you have stairs, keep a heavy object at the base, like a plant or statue.

7. Keep your doors opened whenever possible. A closed door puts limits on energy

8. Don't overfill any area with furniture because cluttered appearance blocks the energy flow.

9. Make sure all the clocks in your house are in working order. A clock that doesn't work symbolizes stagnation since time is standing still. Place a blue or black rug at the front door.

10. Color stimulates mental ability so keep your working environment colorful.

11. Place your desk in a position that gives you a view of the room and the front door.

12. Mirrors can be used here to reflect your path.

13. Write a description of the job you wish to have. Keep it in this area.

14. A green plant or plants in this area symbolizes career growth.

Bagua for Helpful People and Travel

This Bagua area is the Northwestern corner of your home or business. In an individual room, this is the right front section of the Bagua. This location represents the Qi to bring helpful people to our lives. This is also the area representing travel.

Tips to Enhance this Bagua:

White, Gray and Black

1. Use positive affirmations.
2. Keep religious objects, or any symbols of your beliefs, here.
3. Do not sit with your back to the door. If you absolutely must have your back to the door, hang a mirror over your desk to reflect the front door.
4. Keep travel brochures in this area for any destination you hope to travel to and picture yourself at these destinations.

Final Thoughts

These tips are only starting points as you begin Feng Shui.

This book is meant only as basic introduction to the art and science of Feng Shui in simple terms so that anyone can begin to understand and benefit from it. Hopefully it will encourage you to dig deeper and learn more.

A final thing you should be aware of is what is called "poison arrows." These are sharp edges made by objects in the home that are pointed at you by their placement. It can be the edge of a wall that points at your bed, or a table corner pointing in an unfavorable direction. These are examples of what is called the killing breath, which can block the flow of Qi. This creates negative energy for members of the home. The goal of Feng Shui is to cure this.

Most homes with poison arrows can be cured with mirrors, crystals, changing colors and other simple ideas you will have learned in this book.

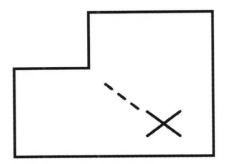

The most common poison arrow is two walls meeting in a sharp angle that points at you in an area where you spend a lot of time. The simplest cure for this is to hang a crystal from the ceiling directly in front of the offending corner. Mirrors can also be hung to deflect negative energy.

Feng Shui is a helpful tool that can increase positive energy and therefore improve our lives. I hope this book inspires you to learn more.

Made in the USA
Middletown, DE
30 June 2020

11653653R00050